About This Book

Title: *Rules*

Step: 4

Word Count: 223

Skills in Focus: Silent e and trigraph dge

Tricky Words: people, follow, keep, signs, builders, pool, fair, laws, world, work

Ideas For Using This Book

Before Reading:
- **Comprehension:** Look at the title and cover image together. Ask readers what they know about rules. What new things do they think they might learn in this book?
- **Accuracy:** Practice saying the tricky words listed on page 1.
- **Phonics:** Write the word *game* on a piece of paper. Point to the pattern *a_e* in the word. Explain that the silent *e* makes the vowel before it have a long sound, saying its own name. Model how to say each sound in the word *game* slowly in isolation. Then, blend the sounds together smoothly to say the whole word. Explain that in some words, such as *rules*, the vowel *u* doesn't say its own name. It makes the /oo/ sound. Offer additional silent *e* examples from the book, such as *make*, *safe*, *line*, and *glide*.
- **Vocabulary:** Briefly explain to readers that a *harness* is a set of straps that attaches a person to something or holds them in place.

During Reading:
- Have readers point under each word as they read it.
- **Decoding:** If readers are stuck on a word, help them say each sound and blend the sounds together smoothly. After reading a sentence, point out words with silent *e* or trigraph *dge* as they appear.
- **Comprehension:** Invite readers to talk about new things they are learning about rules while reading. What are they learning that they didn't know before?

After Reading:
Discuss the book. Some ideas for questions:
- What are some rules that you must follow at different places?
- Why do you think people make rules?

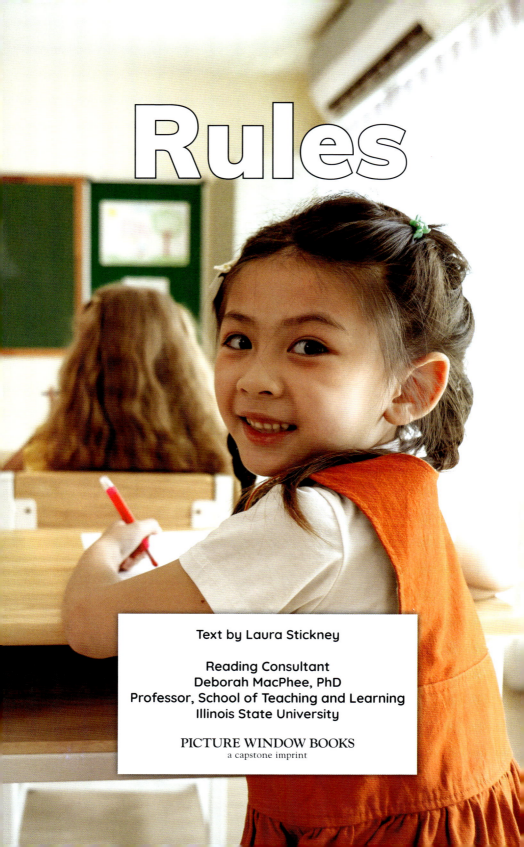

Rules

Text by Laura Stickney

Reading Consultant
Deborah MacPhee, PhD
Professor, School of Teaching and Learning
Illinois State University

PICTURE WINDOW BOOKS
a capstone imprint

What is a rule?

Rules tell people how they must act.

People make rules to keep us safe.

They write rules to make the world work well.

When you drive a car, you must follow rules.

One rule is that cars cannot glide past stop signs.

If a car glides past stop signs, it can strike other cars.

Builders must follow rules when they make a bridge.

One rule is that they must use hard hats. This keeps them safe from things that fall.

They may have to stand on the edge of a ledge or ridge. They must have a harness.

If they slip from the ledge, the harness keeps them safe.

There are rules at places like pools.

The pool deck gets wet.

Kids must not race on it. If they run, they can slip and strike the deck.

The rules give kids a chance to have fun and be safe.

Kids must follow rules at school. These rules keep kids safe.

Kids must not race in halls. If kids race in halls, they can run into other kids.

Games have rules too. In dodge ball, there are rules.

If you get hit, you must sit out. Follow the rules to be fair.

Leaders write rules called laws.

Judges make sure we follow these rules.

Rules make things fair and fun!

More Ideas:

Phonics and Phonemic Awareness Activity

Practicing Silent *e* and Trigraph *dge*:
Play I Spy! Prepare word cards with silent *e* and trigraph *dge* story words. Place each card face up on a surface. Choose a word to start the game. Break apart the sounds and say, "I spy /r/, /u/, /l/" (segment word of choice). The readers will call out the word and then look for the corresponding card. Continue until all cards have been collected. For an extra challenge, have students be the caller, choosing and breaking apart a word.

Suggested words: make, glide, bridge, edge, safe, place, race, line, dodge

Extended Learning Activity

A List of Rules:
Ask readers to think about places they know that have rules, such as their school or a local library. Then help readers draw a chart with columns for each place. Ask readers to list the rules of each place under its corresponding column. Encourage them to use silent *e* or trigraph *dge* words in their list.

Published by Picture Window Books, an imprint of Capstone
1710 Roe Crest Drive, North Mankato, Minnesota 56003
capstonepub.com

Copyright © 2026 by Capstone.
All rights reserved. No part of this publication may be reproduced in whole or in part, or stored in a retrieval system, or transmitted in any form or by any means, electronic, mechanical, photocopying, recording, or otherwise, without written permission of the publisher.

Library of Congress Cataloging-in-Publication Data is available on the Library of Congress website.

ISBN: 9798875227110 (hardback)
ISBN: 9798875230363 (paperback)
ISBN: 9798875230349 (eBook PDF)

Image Credits: iStock: FatCamera, 13, 20–21, kali9, 12, 14, kozmoat98, 15, Richard Stephen, 1, 9, Ridofranz, 22–23, Sviatlana Lazarenka, 25; Shutterstock: alexandre zveiger, 18–19, 32, AnnaStills, 28–29, Bilanol, 10–11, Dennis MacDonald, 4, FamVeld, 30, Hananeko_Studio, 2–3, HighAZ, 5, KOTOIMAGES, 26–27, Monkey Business Images, 24, Prostock-studio, cover, 6–7, Ruslan Lytvyn, 16–17, Suti Stock Photo, 8

Printed and bound in China. 6274